Tellwell Talent
www.tellwell.ca

ISBN
978-0-2288-3159-4 (Hardcover)
978-0-2288-3158-7 (Paperback)

To my boys Ashley, Nathan and Daniel,
here is to more adventures together.
Love Mummy

To my Mother in Love,
thanks for believing in this project.
x Elsie

Two boys I know... brothers really, live in a REMARKABLE HOUSE!
Even more remarkable is their tale of their lived in house.
The adventures they've had in those four walls.
It's a pity there will be no talking from those walls.
So... get those waxy candlesticks out of your ears!
In case you miss something.
Don't be filled with unreasonable fears!
As they tell their tale, learn something.

"There **REALLY** is a CITY in my house!
You don't believe me?
Come on in and I'll show you around.

Four big feet people live here.
My Mum. Dad. brother and I.
We'll show you what we have seen with our own eyes.
We live here all year!
For winter though. we like to escape north to play in the sun!

HIBERNATION is really no fun!

This is Mr Pinchy Bottom, he is an earwig!
I avoid him at all times!

Who wouldn't? See his **BOTTOM SIZE**!!
He likes dark and damp places for sure.
He doesn't like light much.
Maybe his favourite game is hide and seek.
Dad says I shouldn't worry
Mr Pinchy is just shy, he won't bite.

On the wall in the corner, can you see that?
THAT is a Silverfish.
I know what you are thinking!!
How is it a fish when it doesn't live in water?
That's because it is a bug, not an actual fish.
It is silvery in colour and moves like a fish.
I've never actually spoken to any of his kind.

They are always in a **RUSH TO HIDE**.
Maybe we could still become friends.

WATCH OUT for Mrs Leather coat. I've met her my self!

She is a roach and a bit of a scaredy-cat actually.

She tries to hide her egg pods all over the house.

I wish she wouldn't!!

Summer is her favourite.

I really do wish she would live somewhere else

I don't like food she has kissed!

YUCKKK!

This eight-Long-Legged beauty is Ida.
She is really a Daddy-Long-Legs spider.

In winter she just **HANGS ABOUT**, but...
As the weather warms up, her new babies arrive
She needs to weave her web to thrive
On walls, shelves or even indoor plants.
Her bite is harmless to people
Which I'm really glad about.
Wouldn't you?

Meet the most **SWEET TOOTHED FAMILY** I ever met!

Warm weather draws them out.

They march one by one even through net

Neatly in a line, carving a road from their nest to our food.

"Honey? Don't mind if I do!" they say

Oh what stories I could tell!

Just yesterday: Dad forgot to close the honey lid good.

The ants got in, what a gooey mess they got themselves into.

Honeyed ants ANYONE??

Another day I ate a mango and left the pip on the kitchen bench!

What a shock awaited me on my return...

ANTS, ANTS EVERYWHERE!! neatly carting morsels back to their nest.

Dad says when it's cooler they'll go back outside.

See this hole here? Shhhhh! It's a sealed door way.
Birtha, a little mouse lives in there
My mommy is afraid of her!

One day she saw Birtha, and almost **FAINTED** by the door.

Another time she **JUMPED** onto a chair.

She **SCREAMED** so loudly, so early in the morning.
Our neighbours rushed in to rescue her with baseball bats,
Thinking we were being burgled!!
That was funny!!

Now do you believe me?

See… there **REALLY** is a city in my house."

That my friends… is their story.

Until next time…

Did you know?

Ants are social insects and live in big families called colonies.

Ants are one of the strongest and fastest creatures in the animal kingdom. They can carry 50 times their weight. There is this cool one I heard about called the trap jaw ant. It can close its jaws at up to 143 miles per hour (mph), which it uses to kill its prey or injure predators. That is a whopping 2300 times faster than the blink of an eye! Imagine if that ant bit you on your bottom! Ouch! Don't worry though, the ants you might find near your home don't behave like that. Phew!

Silverfish are not really fish. They are given that name because of the way they move and their silvery colour. Silverfish, like living in dark places like cupboards. They are also nocturnal which is why you probably have never seen one.

Cockroaches are some of the oldest insects on the planet. They are very social creatures. Old wives' tales say "if you find one in the open, there is plenty more hiding nearby!".

Daddy-long-legs spiders are tangle web building spiders. That's how they catch food, other insects and even other spiders! They live mostly in urban areas, so in houses or any man-made structures. If you look around your house in ceiling corners, under tables, on or under decks, even in garages and sheds you are bound to find some.

Earwigs are very odd-looking insects with pincers or forceps coming from their bottom. Which is really their tummy. They use those pincers for defence. They look scary but they are not poisonous and do not spread disease.

While mice can look c cute, you don't want mice in your house. They are territorial and will mark their territory by leaving droppings (that's poop) all over your house and weeing in the areas they consider their territory. This could be in your cupboards where you have your food stored. Mummy won't like that one bit! YUCK! They bring diseases some of which can be serious. If you see droppings or mice tracks even in the garage, make sure to tell your parents.

Facts from real life

Photos sourced from Canva

If you have enjoyed reading this book, please leave a review on Amazon. I read every review and they help new readers discover my books. Thank you.

CPSIA information can be obtained
at www.ICGtesting.com
Printed in the USA
BVHW020244310821
615581BV00005BC/244